D1251960

Frank Lloyd Wright's
MARTIN HOUSE COMPLEX

Compiled and written by: Lesley Neufeld
Designer: Vincent Benbenek
Printer: Boncraft

©2004 Martin House Restoration Corporation
All rights reserved
Published in the United States of America

ISBN number 0-9724828-0-6

Darwin D. Martin House Complex
125 Jewett Parkway
Buffalo, New York 14214

Martin House Restoration Corporation
Market Arcade, 617 Main Street
Buffalo, New York 14203
716 856-3858
www.darwinmartinhouse.org

The Martin House Restoration Corporation was formed in 1992.
It is dedicated to restoring Frank Lloyd Wright's five-structure
Darwin D. Martin House Complex to its character as of 1907.
Upon completion of the restoration, the Martin House Complex will
be operated as a historic house museum under the aegis of the New
York State Office of Parks, Recreation and Historic Preservation.

Cover:
Top left: View of Martin House Complex [1903-05] c. 1910
Top right: "Tree of Life" art glass window
Center: Frank Lloyd Wright c. 1905, Darwin D. Martin, 1908
Bottom left: Entry hall in the Martin House
Bottom right: View of the Martin House pergola and
carriage house c. 1910

page 1: The Martin House Complex [1903-05] seen from
Summit Avenue, c. 1910

...the Martin House Complex is a superlative work of Frank Lloyd Wright's Prairie House period.

Frank Lloyd Wright,
[c. 1905] was 36 years
old when he designed
the Martin House

A GREAT ARCHITECT; A GREAT PATRON

Frank Lloyd Wright (1867-1959) was, by all accounts, the greatest American architect. And yet, he was more: a visionary artist and a revolutionary force in the modern culture of the 20th century. Throughout his legendary career, Wright designed hundreds of awe-inspiring buildings, both domestic and commercial; some at grand scale, some more modest.

In the Darwin D. Martin House Complex (1903-1905) Wright had an opportunity to design residences both grand and modest. He created an integrated composition consisting of the magnificent main Martin House (15,000 sq.ft.), the smaller Barton House, built for Martin's sister Delta and her husband, George, a spectacular glass-roofed conservatory linked to the main house by a 100-foot long pergola, a carriage house with chauffeur's apartment above, and finally, in 1908, a gardener's cottage with green-house, all set amid a landscape designed in intricate harmony with the buildings.

Darwin D. Martin [1908]

For his part in the equation, Darwin D. Martin (1865-1935) chose Frank Lloyd Wright as his architect. Martin was, by this time in his life, at the age of 38, a wealthy man, and a senior executive with the Larkin Soap Company of Buffalo. His fore-sight, vision and ambition to have a Wright-designed home for himself and his family, resulted in one of Wright's more unrestrained commissions.

In his 1908 essay, "In the Cause of Architecture," Wright said, I found them [clients] chiefly among American men of business with unspoiled instincts and untainted ideas. A man of this type usually has the faculty of judging for himself."

The special relationship between Martin and Wright resulted in a wealth of correspondence on the design of this residential complex, making it the most completely documented Frank Lloyd Wright commission in existence. Their more than 30-year friendship helped sustain Wright through some economic and emotional hard times. Wright's commission for the Larkin Administration Building (1904-06) and more than 15 other commissions were the product of his long association with Darwin Martin.

When Martin passed away in 1935, Wright corresponded with a colleague and said, "today, my best friend has died." ∎

The Martin House Complex represents Wright at his best – the most advanced expression of his Prairie House concepts.

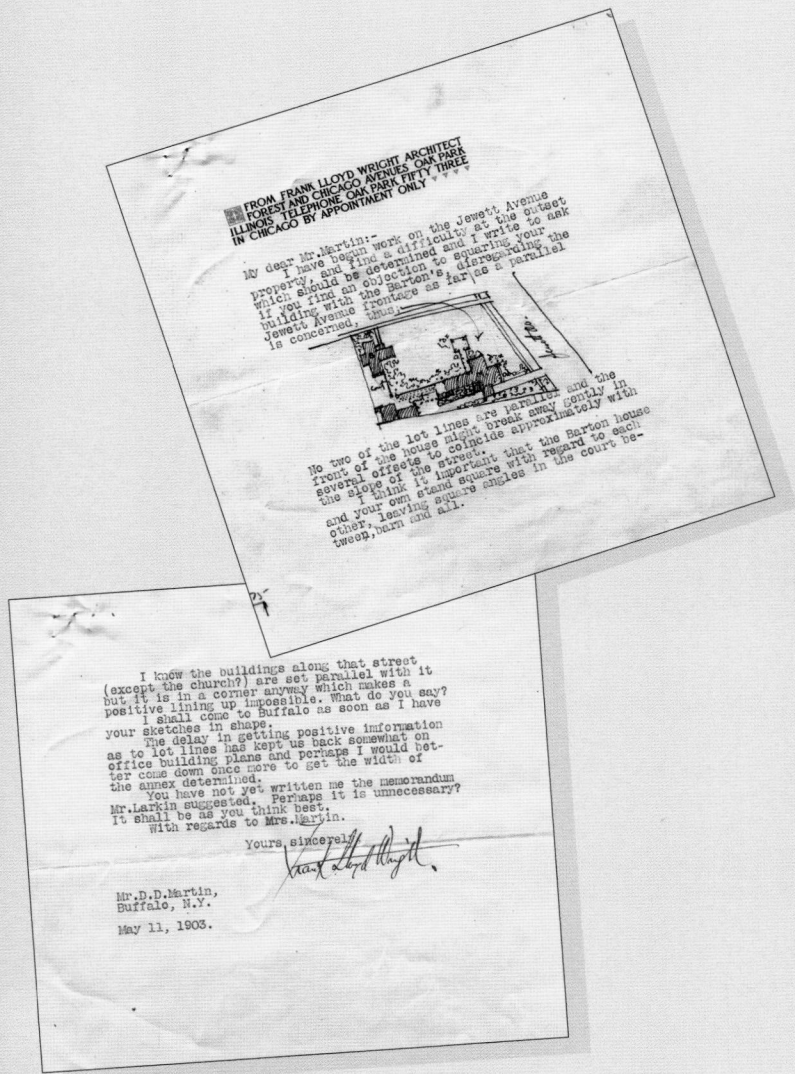

FROM FRANK LLOYD WRIGHT ARCHITECT
FOREST AND CHICAGO AVENUES OAK PARK
ILLINOIS TELEPHONE OAK PARK FIFTY THREE
IN CHICAGO BY APPOINTMENT ONLY

Correspondence from Frank Lloyd Wright to Darwin Martin, May 11, 1903 describing his intention to square the Martin House with the Barton House rather than with the street line of Jewett Parkway.

THE MARTIN HOUSE COMPLEX 1903-05

Frank Lloyd Wright's genius in weaving together structures and landscape, interior and exterior is abundantly evident in the Darwin D. Martin House Complex (1903-05), where each element in the arrangement of five buildings is harmoniously integrated with gardens and grounds.

The Martin House Complex represents the first time in Wright's celebrated career when he had the opportunity to express his genius through a multi-structure composition. Paired with a generous and understanding patron in Darwin Martin, Wright had free rein in conceiving the Complex. The result was an unprecedented work of art of the first order.

Site model (contemporary) of the Martin House Complex.

1. MARTIN HOUSE *(extant)*
2. PERGOLA *(demolished)*
3. CONSERVATORY *(demolished)*
4. BARTON HOUSE *(extant)*
5. CARRIAGE HOUSE/STABLE *(demolished)*

Wright's long, low roofs and intersecting planes nestle down into the landscape, seemingly at one with the earth.

Martin House view from Summit Avenue c.1907

PRAIRIE HOUSE FEATURES

The Martin House Complex exemplifies the Prairie House ideal and the organic principles that Wright developed early in his career. Unlike the vertical stance of the typical Victorian-style homes built in this era, Wright's long, low roofs and intersecting planes nestle down into the landscape seemingly at one with the earth beneath the building.

Although Buffalo, New York is not technically part of the American Prairie, its location in Western New York prompted Wright to extend his theories eastward and declare Buffalo part of the American landscape suitable for a prairie style house.

PRINCIPLES OF THE PRAIRIE HOUSE

■ A CODE TO LIVE AND WORK BY

Early in his career, Frank Lloyd Wright formulated principles by which he set a course for his lifelong design philosophy.

His ideas were set amid late-19th century scholarly thought that championed democracy for its values of liberty and justice. He revered Nature for its organic ability to nurture the spirit and confer contentment upon those who lived within its embrace.

In lectures and articles, such as "A Home in a Prairie Town" for *The Ladies Home Journal,* February 1901, and "In the Cause of Architecture," for *Architectural Record,* Vol XXIII, No. 3, in 1908, he codified the grammar of his work. He defined propositions for how his architecture would create spaces where an American family could find peace and harmony.

A study of the Martin House reveals those principles that guided Wright's work, admirably realized in magnificent architectural form. ▪

During construction, the horizontal planes of the Martin House are apparent in contrast to the existing Victorian houses in the neighborhood, 1904

■ HOMES FOR THE AMERICAN LANDSCAPE

We of the Middle West are living on the prairie. The prairie has a beauty of its own and we should recognize and accentuate this natural beauty, its quiet level. Hence, gently sloping roofs, low proportions, quiet skylines, suppressed heavy-set chimneys and sheltering overhangs, low terraces and out-reaching walls sequestering private gardens.

— FRANK LLOYD WRIGHT
IN THE CAUSE OF ARCHITECTURE,
ARCHITECTURAL RECORD,
VOL. XXIII, NO. 3, 1908

Although the evolutionary steps toward a fully-developed Prairie House are seen in Wright's earlier houses, the Martin House, with its conservatory, pergola, carriage house and integrated landscape, is a truly mature rendition of the theoretical model Wright proposed.

All of the unique Prairie House features are splendidly illustrated in the Martin House. Its low profile nestles quietly into the site under a gently sloping roof; the strong mass of chimney anchors the building at the cross-axial heart of the interior plan; the long, gentle roof planes reach out to shelter the gardens and accentuate the restful horizontal lines of the House; banded windows dissolve the traditional barriers between interior and exterior; and the broadly based foundation gives the illusion that the building is one with the ground that supports it. ▪

Illustration from "A Home in a Prairie Town" by Frank Lloyd Wright, *The Ladies Home Journal,* February 1901

BREAKING THE BOX

Wright was determined to vanquish the "boxed-in" interiors common to Victorian residential architecture, believing that such environments were detrimental to a person's well being. An early step in his evolution of this idea is found in the Barton House where Wright "breaks" the corner of the building on the second floor. His use of banded windows wrapping the corners on the upper story obscures the distinction between interior and exterior space.

He develops the "breaking the box" idea further in the Martin House with even more emphatic bands of windows and with the cross-axial interior plan that pushes corners of rooms outward into the landscape.

> Wright was determined to vanquish the "boxed-in" interiors common to Victorian residential architecture, believing that such environments were detrimental to a person's well being.

CROSS-AXIAL PLAN

Wright organized the spaces of the Martin House Complex with a series of axial lines that intersect like spines connecting the entire composition. The east-west axis that aligns the Barton House, conservatory, carriage house and related gardens is intersected by the powerful north-south axis that runs from the Martin House entrance, along the pergola and concludes at the conservatory where it transects the east-west line. Two other axes cross in the living room; one east-west that leads the eye eastward out to the veranda and garden, and another on the north-south axis that heads northward to the gardens flanking the pergola.

The sense of flow explicit in these intersections implies a symbolic representation of progress and motion. The cruciform interior plan spirals around these intersections creating open space to seemingly reflect the interactions of the modern American family.

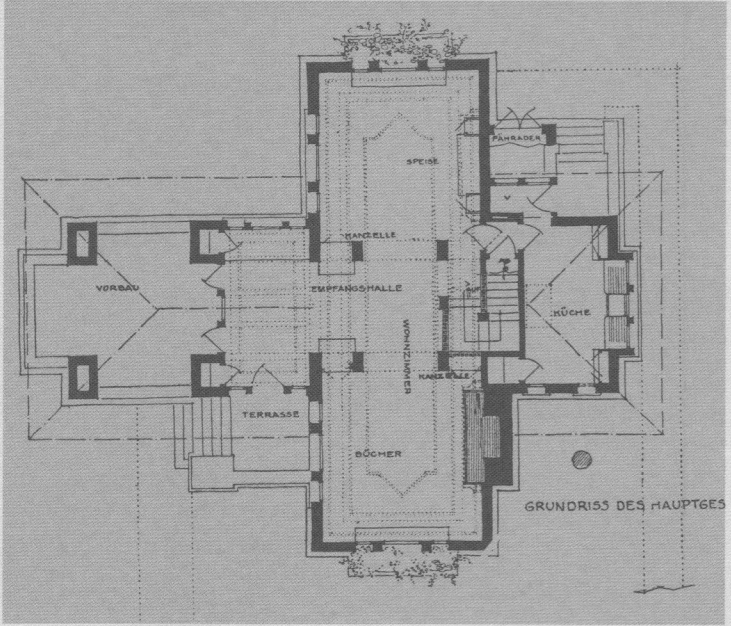

Plan of the George Barton House as it was published in Germany in the *Wasmuth* portfolio, 1910.

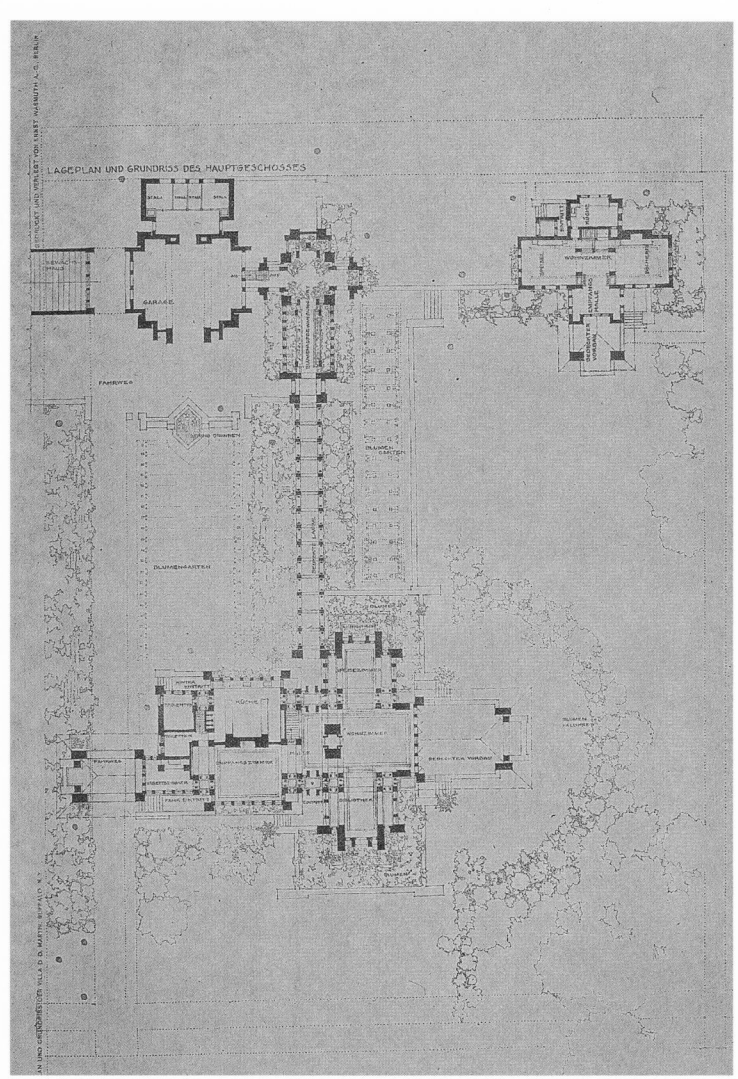

Site plan of the Martin House from the *Wasmuth* portfolio published in Germany in 1910.

■ FREE FLOWING SPACE; OPEN PLAN

The ground plan, which is intended to explain itself, is arranged to offer the least resistance to a simple mode of living, in keeping with a high ideal of family life together.

— A HOME IN A PRAIRIE TOWN,
THE LADIES HOME JOURNAL,
FEBRUARY, 1901

Wright designed modern domestic environments for modern American families. He denounced the boxy interiors of the typical Victorian homes planted onto the American landscape. Instead, his Prairie Houses were designed to "break the box;" to tear down the interior walls that created rooms, thus giving people freedom to move and families a better opportunity to interact with one another.

The Martin House plan portrays this principle splendidly. The cruciform plan is devised to allow functional spaces to flow one into the other, delineated not by interior walls, but by the structural elements: pier clusters and ceiling beams; and by subtle devices such as frieze rails, and ceiling moldings. Always these spaces expand beyond their sheltering walls to the outside by Wright's attention to windows placed everywhere — even some to allow views from one interior space to the outside and then back again to an interior beyond.

Wright communicated his intention for spaces to be used for movement or repose by how he manipulated the interior structure. He lowered ceilings to speed passage through one area only to release the space in the next to dramatize arrival. He enclosed other spaces with subtle architectural gestures to provide places for rest and contemplation. He turned the staircase in a series of landings to create transition between public and private spaces.

In the great expanse of space called the unit room, he used ceiling height changes, frieze rails, pier clusters, windows and furnishings together to define intimate gathering spaces, such as in the dining room, living room and library, all organized around spaces that flow between them to suggest movement and traffic patterns. ■

The 100-foot pergola was a remarkable walkway intended by Wright to unify the arrangement of buildings on the site...

Conservatory with *Nike of Samothrace* at the focal point of the central organizing axis of the Martin House, 1907.

View from the Martin House front entry looking down pergola, 1907.

PERGOLA

An astonishing and dramatic perspective greeted visitors who stepped through the Martin House foyer and looked toward the conservatory. The 100-foot pergola was a remarkable walkway intended by Wright to unify the arrangement of buildings on the site and connect the main house with the indoor gardens of the conservatory.

CONSERVATORY

The glazed, sun-lit conservatory that Wright designed for the Martin House formed the thematic center of the entire composition. Here, a replica of the *Nike of Samothrace,* (The Winged Victory,) graced the focal niche surrounded by lush interior plantings. Wright used this particular sculpture in many of his early buildings, but here its undeniable elegance and power provided a graceful counterpoint to the relentless rectilinearity of the Martin House composition.

In 1910, Berlin publisher, Ernst Wasmuth, published a series of Wright's drawings, including the Martin House Complex, in the *Wasmuth Portfolio Ausgeführte Bauten und Entwürfe von Frank Lloyd Wright*. This publication presented Wright's work to European architects for the first time. His influence on the emerging modernist design movement was immense for here he presented modern buildings that embodied courageous concepts such as form following function.

■ UNIFIED WITH NATURE

Primarily, Nature furnished the architectural motifs out of which the architectural forms as we know them today have been developed, and although our practice for centuries has been for the most part to turn from her, seeking inspiration in books and adhering slavishly to dead formulae, her wealth of suggestion is inexhaustible; her riches greater than any man's desire.

> – FRANK LLOYD WRIGHT
> IN THE CAUSE OF ARCHITECTURE,
> ARCHITECTURAL RECORD,
> VOL. XXIII, NO. 3, 1908

Wright believed that the predominantly European house styles found in 19th and early-20th century America, with their powerful vertical rooflines and ornate, applied decorations, were unsuitable affronts to the American landscape and sensibilities. His propositions for a truly American architecture were based upon the values and ideals of late-19th century scholarly thinking that sought harmony with Nature for the betterment of all society.

Unlike the Victorian era homes in the neighborhood, the horizontal roofs of the Martin House send out their great cantilevered eaves like branches to gather in portions of the surrounding landscape. The House huddles low on the site and is at rest with its surroundings suggesting harmony with the earth beneath it. ■

■ DESIGNED FROM WITHIN

"The spaces within are the great truth about the building."

> – FRANK LLOYD WRIGHT

Wright believed that interior spaces, more than the exterior forms of architecture, provided the defining reality of a building, the essential elements that would create the experience of habitation. He designed from within; meaning that he envisioned livable, interior space and allowed walls and roof to enclose those spaces.

Always, the landscape was woven into the interior experience. Wright arranged the Martin House plan to frame the trees and gardens beyond the walls and windows, each space open to views outside, artfully giving landscape features a presence within. Interior rooms flow from one into the other in intricate, orchestrated intersections of spaces and vistas.

The abstract patterns in the art-glass windows, or "light screens" as Wright referred to them, filter exterior views with stylized nature-forms so that the viewer is reminded once again of the relationship between indoors and out.

Gardens take on the character of outdoor rooms, so framed and formed by the patterns of the interior plan. ■

Darwin D. Martin, at 38 years of age, was a self-made millionaire by the time he met Frank Lloyd Wright in 1902.

Darwin D. Martin, 1908.

Isabelle Reidpath Martin, c 1910.

DARWIN AND ISABELLE MARTIN

Darwin and Isabelle Martin were married June 26, 1889. Their first house was in the same neighborhood where they eventually built their Wright-designed home. Wright assisted the Martins in choosing the expansive vacant lot at the corner of Jewett Parkway and Summit Avenue, that could accommodate a large estate.

Their correspondence reveals that Darwin Martin was Wright's principal client for the commission. Isabelle, his wife, took a less participatory role, but offered opinions and objections, mostly conveyed through her husband's letters.

The Martin Family, c. 1907, posed in the garden next to the pergola. Darwin is in the center with Isabelle seated, reading with her children, their young son Darwin R. Martin, center front and their daughter Dorothy with white bows in her hair. The rest are Isabelle's relatives.

Pergola view toward conservatory, 1907.

■ A PORTRAYAL OF THE OWNER

*I try to make each house char-
acteristic of its owner always and
an interpretation when possible.*

*That individuality in a building
was possible for each housemaker,
or desirable, seemed at that time
to rise to the dignity of an idea.*

> – FRANK LLOYD WRIGHT
> IN THE CAUSE OF ARCHITECTURE,
> ARCHITECTURAL RECORD,
> VOL. XXIII, NO. 3, 1908

Entering the Martin House was a dramatic event. From the low threshold, guests
would feel the powerful release of space sweeping up to the second floor staircase
while simultaneously their view would be drawn down the 100-foot pergola towards
the lush gardens within the conservatory, 1907.

Darwin Martin's life story
presented Wright with
metaphorical raw materials
for interpreting his client in
the Martin House Complex.
The circumstances of Martin's
youth: the loss of his mother
at an early age, separation from
his father and siblings, and a
life of hard work that began at
age 13, created in him a heartfelt
desire to reunite his fragmented
family to live together again in
close proximity.

Darwin Martin eventually rose
to great fortune and social
position with the Larkin Soap
Company, in Buffalo, New York.
By 1902, when he met Frank
Lloyd Wright, Martin was a mil-
lionaire executive with a wife
and young children of his own
and an ambition to make
amends for his days as a lonely,

struggling child living in isola-
tion from his family. These two
ambitions of Martin's fueled
Wright's creation of an integrated complex of buildings and
gardens for Martin and his kin.

Wright described his architecture
as appealing to "American men
of business." This characteriza-
tion seemed to fit Darwin
Martin who may well have
been attracted to the radical
"differentness" of Wright's
designs as a means to express
his own character and status in
the community. In 1902, his
brother, William, appealed to
Darwin in a letter, saying, "he
[Wright] will build you the finest
house in Buffalo – you will be
the envy of every rich man in
Buffalo and it will be published
in all the Buffalo newspapers." ■

> "...the most perfect thing of its kind in the world
> – a domestic symphony, true, vital, comfortable."
> – Frank Lloyd Wright

UNITY AND HARMONY

Frank Lloyd Wright lavished his attention on every detail of the Martin House. When he was done, he pinned the site plan to his drawing board and kept it there for nearly 50 years. In 1954, when an architect named Sebastian Tauriello purchased the Martin House, Wright wrote to him to say, "treat the opus according to its merits."

Wright's reference to the Martin House as his "opus" recalls his fondness for musical metaphors and a letter to Darwin Martin (October 13, 1904) when he promises that he will not rest until "DDM has the most perfect thing of its kind in the world – a domestic symphony, true, vital, comfortable."

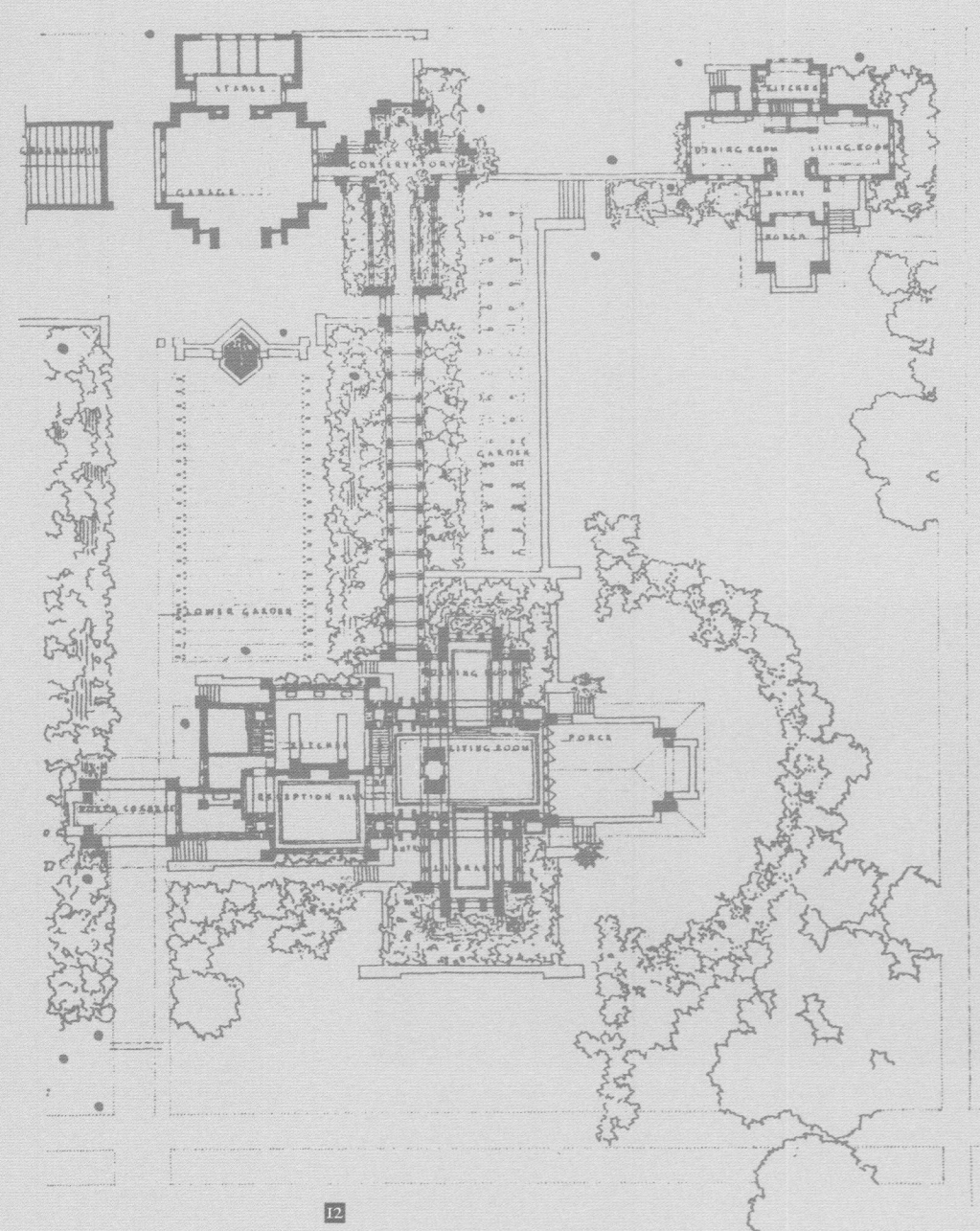

Plan drawing of the Martin House Complex as presented by Frank Lloyd Wright for the *Wasmuth* portfolio published in Germany in 1910.

■ DESIGNED FROM A UNIFIED IDEA

The differentiation of a simple form characterizes the expression of one building. Quite a different form may serve for another, but from one basic idea all the formal elements of design are in each case derived and held well together in scale and character.

— FRANK LLOYD WRIGHT
IN THE CAUSE OF ARCHITECTURE,
ARCHITECTURAL RECORD,
VOL. XXIII, NO. 3, 1908

Wright's Prairie Houses share a consistent language of elements in their horizontal profiles, anchoring chimney masses, broad-based foundations and overhanging eaves. But each also contains unique characteristics related specifically to contexts of site and owner. Wright selected central "motifs" or ideas, from which all details would flow, thus creating a harmonious composition of elements.

Wright promised Darwin Martin "a domestic symphony." This concept seems to be born out as a musical motif in the intricate harmonies of the Martin House plan. Looking at the plan (page 12), rhythms are suggested by the balance and repetition of solid shapes, (equivalent to musical notes,) with spatial voids, (analogous to pauses or rests in music.) Wright composed the pier and structural elements of various proportions of size and scale to relate to one another in a measured arrangement that is highly balanced and symphonic in character ■

View of the Martin House Complex from atop a neighboring house, looking northeast, c.1907

QUARTER-SAWN OAK

Wright specified quarter-sawn oak to be used extensively for woodwork and furnishings throughout the Martin House. In this method, oak logs are split into four quarters and then cut from the center of the tree outward on a diagonal. The result is a very fine grain in the finished product and greater strength than what results from plain-sawn lumber. Because quarter-sawing yields less lumber per tree than plain-sawing and is more labor-intensive, it is a method that is little used today. In the early part of the 20th century, however, it was a hallmark feature of fine craft in both Prairie School and Arts and Crafts furnishings and woodwork.

Famed "Tree of Life" window at the Martin House staircase (contemporary photograph).

"Bring out the nature in the materials...Reveal the nature of the wood, plaster, brick or stone in your designs; they are all by nature friendly and beautiful."
– Frank Lloyd Wright

View toward Martin House across the kitchen garden, c. 1910.

■ NATURAL COLORS AND MATERIALS

*Go to the woods and the fields
for color schemes.*

*Bring out the nature of the
materials; let their nature
intimately into your scheme.*

– FRANK LLOYD WRIGHT
IN THE CAUSE OF ARCHITECTURE,
ARCHITECTURAL RECORD,
VOL. XXIII, NO. 3, 1908

Wright believed that the colors
of nature, "the soft, warm,
optimistic tones of earth and
autumn leaves" would create a
more harmonious domestic
environment than would the
fabricated colors from synthetic
dyes and pigments that were
more characteristic of the
Victorian style homes of the day.

Materials, such as wood, brick,
plaster and stone were to him,
"all by nature friendly and
beautiful." He required only to
reveal these surface textures –
raw materials from the earth
finished to bring out their intrinsic character.

For the Martin House, Wright
selected golden yellow Roman
bricks, terra cotta roof tiles,
earth-brown ceramic floor tiles,
and quarter-sawn yellow oak
of a rich, amiable hue. These
same materials flowed from
outside to inside, drawing the
eye from the rooms within to
the world without, creating an
illusion that the interior and
Nature were one.

Colors and materials together
created a warm, golden glow
throughout the Martin House.
These were enhanced even
more emphatically by autumnal
tones in the exquisitely tinted
panes of Wright-designed art
glass windows, and by golden
bronze painted over mortar
joints in between interior bricks.
Sunshine through colored
glass by day, and hearth-fire's
light reflected in gold mortar
cast the interior of the Martin
House with an amber glow. ■

Wright intended anyone within the house to look outdoors through the artful device of his art glass patterns, and become aware of the neighboring treetops, the beauty of filtered sunlight, and color in the garden.

The pattern that became known as "Tree of Life" after Wight's lifetime was located in the Martin House reception room on the main floor, and throughout the rooms of the second floor.

WINDOWS

Each of the art glass "light screens," as Wright called the windows, doors and skylights in the Martin House, is endowed with Wright's genius in creating decorative abstract patterns.

The Martin House "Tree of Life" windows, though not named as such by Frank Lloyd Wright are among the most revered of Wright's art glass designs. Each full window contains more than 700 individual pieces of glass set into brass "caming." These tiny panes of glass reflect sunlight from their iridescent surfaces on the exterior of the Martin House while filtering light to the interior through green and golden hues. Leaves of the treetops outside are seen through the abstract filter of Wright's stylized pattern, reminding the viewer to be conscious of nature beyond.

The original requisitions for manufacturing the Martin House Complex windows went to the Linden Glass Company of Chicago.

In a fine art sense these designs have grown as natural plants grow, the individuality of each is integral and as complete as skill, time strength and circumstances would permit.

The method in itself does not of necessity produce a beautiful building, but it does provide a framework as a basis which has an organic integrity, susceptible to the architect's imagination and at once opening to him Nature's wealth of artistic suggestion, ensuring him a guiding principle within which he can never be wholly false, out of tune, or lacking in rational motif.

— FRANK LLOYD WRIGHT
IN THE CAUSE OF ARCHITECTURE,
ARCHITECTURAL RECORD,
VOL. XXIII, NO. 3, 1908

■ GEOMETRY DRAWN FROM NATURE

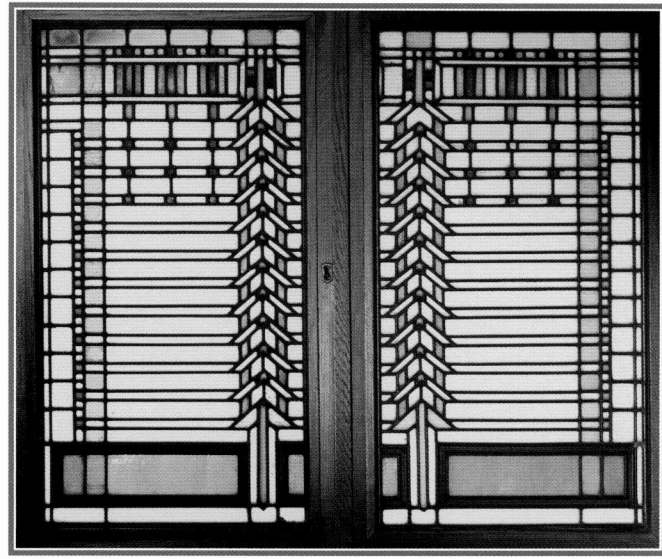

Pier cluster windows.

Conservatory window.

What architectural decoration the buildings carry is not only conventionalized to the point where it is quiet and stays as a sure foil for the nature forms from which it is derived – but it is always of the surface and never on it.

— FRANK LLOYD WRIGHT
IN THE CAUSE OF ARCHITECTURE,
ARCHITECTURAL RECORD,
VOL. XXIII, NO. 3, 1908

The intricate, abstract geometry of which Wright was a master is beautifully illustrated in the varieties of art glass windows found in the Martin House.

Looking out from within the house, one views the landscape outside through vertical planes that have patterns suggestive of trees, shrubs or vines, such as the wisteria that grew along the Martin House pergola. Wright intended this use of natural foliage, not as surface decoration, but as integral to his concept of harmonizing interior space with the landscape beyond.

Art glass panels in the horizontal plane were used in skylights and lay-lights (covers over electric lights) throughout the house. Designs for these echo geometries found in Wright's floor plan for the Complex. ■

Window in the Martin House living room, dining room and library in the "Wisteria" pattern.

Martin House reception room, 1907 showing the barrel chairs and "sunburst" fireplace.

FIREPLACES

Metaphorically, Wright thought of the fireplace as the unifying heart of the home. For the Martin House he created, with the help of talented craftsmen, a most magnificent heart: a glorious two-sided fireplace that greeted visitors in the entry hall and warmed the family in the living room. The chimney mass was clad on all four sides with a glass mosaic depicting wisteria vines with green leaves veined in gold and interspersed with purple blossoms cascading downward onto brownish-gold tiles. Orlando Giannini, who Wright introduced to Darwin Martin by saying, "he is cracker-jack," created the fireplace.

The fireplace in the reception room featured a semi-circle of brick arranged in a "sunburst" effect around the hearth. Wright assigned symbolism to shapes, the circle representing infinity, so the fireplace in this room takes on deeper meaning as a unifying heart of the home. The fireplace glow was made richer by the use of bronze gilding in the mortar joints between the bricks.

THE UNIT ROOM

The great expanse of space called the "unit room" dramatically illustrates Wright's achievement in open planning in the Martin House. Wright put his familiarity with concrete and steel "skyscraper" technology to use in opening up the main living areas of the house to allow the flow of one space into another. The dining room, living room and library are joined without interior walls as one unit of space, but are delineated more subtly by Wright's use of three design elements: pier clusters at the corners of each "room," woodwork moldings on the ceilings and dropped frieze rails that join each space.

The front hall fireplace [detail] created a glistening focal point in the entry, 1907.

Wright put his familiarity with concrete and steel "skyscraper" technology to use in opening up the main living areas of the house to allow the flow of one space into another.

■ SIMPLICITY AND REPOSE

Simplicity and Repose are qualities that measure the true value of any work of art.

— FRANK LLOYD WRIGHT
IN THE CAUSE OF ARCHITECTURE,
ARCHITECTURAL RECORD,
VOL. XXIII, NO. 3, 1908

For Wright and many of his contemporary scholars in this era, home represented a place for spiritual renewal. Victorian clutter and decorative styles were seen as incompatible with a sense of repose and were thought to be contrary to modern domestic life. A house, they believed, ought to provide the center for family life, harmonious and simple in detail to create a peaceful atmosphere. It ought to be easy to care for and decorated only with artful things thought to be useful and beautiful.

The artfulness with which Wright created the Martin House Complex is testament to this principle. Throughout the design of the Martin House is evidence of the simplicity that Wright advocated for achieving a sense of repose. "As few rooms as will meet the conditions which give it rise and under which we live," he declared, "really there need be but one room, the living room with requirements otherwise sequestered from it or screened within by means of architectural contrivances." The great "unit room" of the Martin House, encompassing dining room, living room and library, is such a room as Wright describes, open and simple, where "comfort and utility may go hand in hand with beauty."

Decoration is kept minimal and harmonized so that "it means something good in the scheme as a whole." Storage and furnishings are built-in, "considering the whole as an integrated unit." ■

The Martin House living room, the intimate seating area in the expansive "unit room," 1907.

Darwin D. Martin with his children: son, Darwin Reidpath Martin and daughter, Dorothy Reidpath Martin, 1907.

The Martin House dining room, 1907. The high-back chairs and unique table design, created an intimate space-within-in-a-space concept.

A corner stanchion, purchased at auction and returned to the Martin House, shows candles instead of the electric lamps Wright designed.

DINING TABLE

Frank Lloyd Wright designed a unique dining table for the Martin House that echoed other design themes in the architecture of the house. Originally, it was shaped as a letter "I" with projecting corners that surrounded diners at the table in a "room within a room." Mounted on each corner were four "stanchions," each designed to hold a planter and four small lamps. These corner lamps, illuminated floral arrangements below and bathed those seated at the table in a warm glow.

The Martins had the stanchions removed after awhile as they proved awkward, getting in the way of dining and serving.

PIER CLUSTERS

Concealing mechanical functions, such as heating, was an important principle behind Wright's design for the fittings in the Martin House. Pier clusters, the structural support elements for the house, double as clever design devices that hide radiant heating units and create storage opportunities for the Martins' extensive collection of books. Art-glass windows at the top of these "radiators" swung open to allow heat to flow into the rooms and provide views from one space into another.

Martin House Library pier cluster, 1907.

■ TOTAL DESIGN, INTEGRATED DETAILS

*It is quite impossible to consider
the building one thing and its
furnishings another.*
— FRANK LLOYD WRIGHT 1910

*One thing instead of many
things. A great thing instead of
a collection of smaller ones.*

*I believe a house is more a home
for being a work of art.*
— FRANK LLOYD WRIGHT 1932

Wright is renowned for design-
ing "total" environments.
As much attention to detail went into his furnishings and
decorative components as into
the spaces and structure.
Always the goal was to create
harmony between all design
elements in the composition –
thus, a unified whole.

For the Martin House, Wright
designed numerous pieces
of furniture, notable among
them, the barrel chair. He
subsequently modified the
design of this chair for Taliesin,
his home in Wisconsin, for
the Herbert F. Johnson House,
"Wingspread" in Racine,
Wisconsin and for Fallingwater
in Bear Run, Pennsylvania. But
in the Martin House, the circular
form of his famous chair echoes
the semi-circle he used for the
reception room fireplace and
the floricycle in the garden.

The high-back chairs and
distinctive capital letter "I" –
shaped dining table are another
example of highly specific design
that was intended to harmonize
with other Martin House
interior detailing and ideas.

BARREL CHAIR
The first barrel chair ever designed
by Wright was for the Martin
House. It became a favored design
that he used with various modifica-
tions in later commissions, including
Fallingwater and his own home,
Taliesin. The round shapes in the
barrel chair, echoed in the semi-cir-
cles of the reception room fireplace
and the "floricycle" in the garden,
interject the softening influence
of the circle into the predominantly
rectilinear composition of the
Martin House.

Wright lavished his creative
genius on the Martin House
details; all elements were
designed as harmonious parts
of an overall composition.
Design continuity pervades
throughout Wright's composition
with the repetition of shapes and
forms in art-glass light screens,
wood trims, furniture, lamps and
structural details. ■

The fireplace, [which is double-faced and also open to the entry hall]
creates a focal point in the Martin House living room, circa 1907.

"A building should appear to grow easily from its site..."
– Frank Lloyd Wright

View of the carriage house, conservatory, with bird houses atop, and pergola, overlooking the Martin House kitchen garden, 1907.

WISTERIA AND GINKGO

Delicate wisteria vines and flamboyant ginkgo leaves have become enduring symbols for the Martin House, calling attention, as Frank Lloyd Wright intended, to elements from nature.

Two ginkgo trees, chosen by Wright, were planted as sentinels on either side of the Martin House driveway. In autumn, their swirling leaves turn to a yellow-gold color that matches almost exactly the Roman brick that Wright specified for the house. Ginkgo trees were a favorite of Wright's — he specified their planting in several other of his landscape designs.

Wisteria vines were planted next to the Martin House pergola. Their dainty purple blossoms became the inspiration for the glass mosaic on the entry hall fireplace (shown on previous page) and the art-glass pattern Wright created for the unit room windows and veranda doors.

Martin House urns, c.1907.

URNS

Garden elements were intrinsic to the holistic design approach that Wright took to the Martin House Complex. Decorative urns, cascading with greenery and flowers, stood on pier columns and railings, some hiding entrances, where they were intended to integrate structure with nature. Wright's attention to detail is truly demonstrated by the fact that grids of indented squares that decorate the urns exactly match grids of projecting squares on the birdhouses.

BIRDHOUSES

Frank Lloyd Wright's wry sense of humor comes into play in his design for the Martin House birdhouses, placed as finials on the roof of the conservatory. Intended as multi-family dwellings for Purple Martens, Wright's design presents an obvious play-on-words on the Martin family name. As always, Wright's attention to detail shines through as he harmonized these decorative elements with similar forms throughout the Complex. It is unlikely that these birdhouses ever functioned as planned, since Martens tend to live near water and the stone construction would have created too over-heated an environment for the birds.

GARDENS AND GROUNDS – FLORICYCLE

Frank Lloyd Wright designed the Martin House Complex gardens and grounds with a characteristically unified, holistic approach in order to harmonize buildings and landscape. Garden elements are visible from every window throughout the Complex. The extensive landscape design provided Isabelle Martin, Darwin's wife, an avid gardener, with numerous grand flowerbeds where she nurtured shrubs and perennials of all assortments.

Frank Lloyd Wright intended a sweeping arc for the east side of the Martin House veranda – which he referred to as a "hemicycle" and Martin called the "floricycle" – planted with shrubs and flowers that would produce an array of blooms to offer color throughout the spring and summer.

View of the pergola and east gardens, c.1910.

■ INTEGRATED WITH THE SITE

A building should appear to grow easily from its site and be shaped to harmonize with its surroundings if Nature is manifest there, and if not to try to make it as quiet, substantial and organic as She would have been if the opportunity were Hers.

— FRANK LLOYD WRIGHT
IN THE CAUSE OF ARCHITECTURE,
ARCHITECTURAL RECORD,
VOL. XXIII, NO. 3, 1908

Gardens, grounds and exterior elements are intrinsic to the holistic approach to design that characterizes Wright's work. This is especially true in the Martin House Complex landscape design where the natural elements are so interwoven with the structural design.

The Martin House landscape is framed by views from inside to out, each as an extension of the living spaces within. The extensive gardens furnished the complex with numerous grand flowerbeds filled with perennials, shrubs and annuals of all assortments.

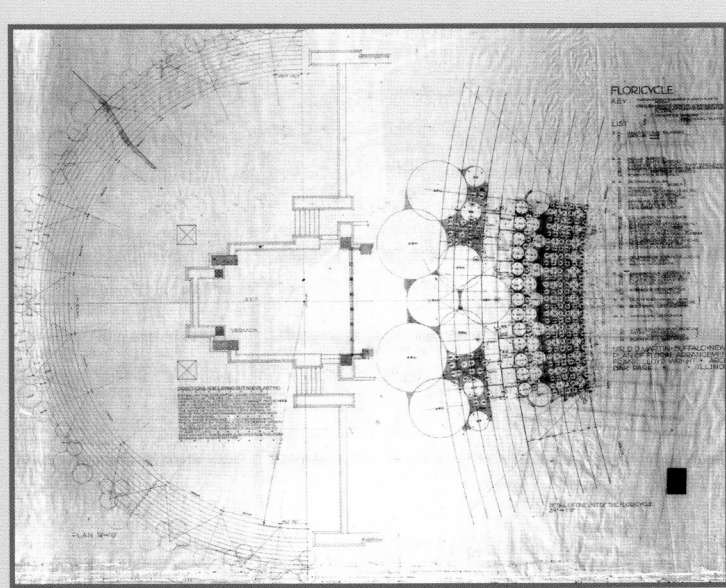

Plan and detail of the "floricycle" for the Martin House gardens, drawn by Walter Burley Griffin, the landscape architect who worked for Frank Lloyd Wright.

View looking west from the Carriage House toward the greenhouse and rear of the Gardener's Cottage. Mrs. Martin [foreground] and daughter Dorothy are shown at left in the hedge, c. 1920.

...the Barton House stands as a gem on its own; a fine example of a modest, mid-size residential design in the early evolutionary stages of Wright's Prairie House style.

THE FIRST BUFFALO COMMISSION

THE GEORGE BARTON HOUSE - 1903

Frank Lloyd Wright's first commission in Buffalo was to design a house for Darwin Martin's sister, Delta, and her husband, George Barton, a Larkin Soap Company employee. The project was intended as "an experiment" in which client and architect could assess their working relationship and Wright could demonstrate his worthiness for the larger assignments Martin had in mind, namely his own residence and the Larkin Administration Building.

Martin chose a design for the George Barton House borrowed directly from Wright's previous design for the J.J. Walser House (1902) in Chicago. Wright's alter-ations to the earlier work, such as the selection of golden yellow Roman brick and terra cotta roof tiles, anticipate the look and feel of the entire Martin House Complex

The George Barton House, c. 1910.

Even prior to completion of the Barton House, Martin commissioned Wright to design the next phases of work that would include the carriage house, conservatory, pergola and the main Martin House (1903-05).

A cruciform interior plan, a veranda thrust into the landscape, art-glass windows, and Prairie House features – broad overhanging eaves, banded windows, low-hipped roofs, and horizontal emphasis – harmonize the Barton House with the design of the Martin

House Complex. Yet, the Barton House stands as a gem on its own; a fine example of a modest, mid-size residential design in the early evolutionary stages of Wright's Prairie House form.

Wright designed fixtures and furnishings specifically for the Barton House, including jewel-like wall sconces and pendant lights, and a built-in sideboard for the dining room in which the iridescent surfaces of the delicately patterned art-glass doors glimmer with reflected light.

Frank Lloyd Wright's Larkin Administration Building, built 1904-06, Buffalo, New York, 1907.

THE LARKIN BUILDING

Darwin Martin's patronage resulted in Wright's Larkin Administration Building as well as ten other commisssions, over the span of their 33-year friendship.

Wright claimed in his book, *An American Architecture*, 1955, that he "first consciously began to try to beat the box" in the Larkin Building. The famed Buffalo landmark was his first commercial commission, won for him through Darwin Martin's influence. It was demolished in 1950. Yet, in its day, it was a revolutionary work in a brave new world of architectural design that was destined to become one of the most important works of the 20th century.

For the health and benefit of Larkin Company employees, Wright designed an interior environment with a soaring, open atrium, awash in natural light flooding in from skylights, and vine-draped tiers. Employees and executives alike worked at their desks in an open floor plan that was intended to reflect democratic ideals. Declarative mottos inscribed into the balconies were meant to inspire and uplift their spirits throughout the day. Wright's building design was conducive to comfort and health throughout. Many innovative features were implemented for the first time in the Larkin Building such as air conditioning and wall-hung water closets and partitions.

But even beyond such modern conveniences, the Larkin Building featured innovations in work place environments such as a rooftop restaurant and roofdeck, a conservatory under the skylights for plants, a library, infirmary, classroom, YWCA room and lounges.

...it was a revolutionary work in a brave new world of architectural design that was destined to become one of the most important works of the 20th century.

The William R. Heath House (1905-06) (contemporary photograph).

■ HOMES FOR EVERYONE

"There should be as many kinds (styles) of houses as there as kinds (styles) of people and as many differentiations as there are different individuals. A man who has individuality...has a right to its expression in his own environment"

— FRANK LLOYD WRIGHT
IN THE CAUSE OF ARCHITECTURE,
ARCHITECTURAL RECORD,
VOL. XXIII, NO. 3, 1908

Frank Lloyd Wright's legacy in Western New York provides examples of houses designed for a variety of "lifestyles" and income levels. Wright designed a substantial home in Buffalo for Larkin Company executive, William R. Heath, in 1905-06, and a more modest home for Larkin employee, Walter V. Davidson in 1908-09. On the Martin House Complex there is the grand main house for Darwin Martin, the mid-size George Barton House, an apartment for the chauffeur, and a cottage (1909) for the Martin House gardener. In 1926-27, the Martins had Wright design their summer home, called Graycliff, in Derby, New York.

The Walter V. Davidson House (1908-09) (contemporary photograph).

Graycliff, the Martin family summer home (1926-27), in Derby, New York, c.1930.

GRAYCLIFF

Isabelle Martin became Wright's client for the commission to build a summer home for the family on a 70-foot cliff overlooking Lake Erie just south of Buffalo. At Graycliff (1926-27), Wright created an airy, light-filled, open plan with an "organic" architectural vocabulary that he based upon references to the rocky shoreline. Abundantly detailed with windows and patio doors opening onto sun-bathed terraces, the 6,500 square-foot house captures cool lake breezes and warm summer sunlight. Cantilevered balconies allow for spectacular views over the lake.

GARDENER'S COTTAGE

Wright completed the Martin House Complex composition in 1908-09 with the addition of a Gardener's Cottage (extant) thoughtfully located a few steps from the Martin House gardens. The cottage is wood-frame construction with a stucco finish and cedar trim, rather than the Roman brick of the Martin and Barton Houses, and has a cozy, compact plan on two floors.

Darwin Martin purchased a new carriage and team of horses shortly after the family moved into the house in 1905.

CARRIAGE HOUSE

Wright's plan for the Martin House Complex included a rather spacious carriage house with stables and an apartment above for the coachman (later a garage with chauffeur's quarters). Wright echoed the structural design features of the main Martin House and created an art-glass pattern for the carriage house windows using a series of squares and rectangles that resonates with the "Tree of Life" windows from the Martin House.

The carriage house viewed from across the kitchen garden, c. 1912.

The Gardener's Cottage (1909) (contemporary photograph).

Work began on the Martin House in 1903. The Martin family moved into their new house in November 1905. Craftsmen continued to work on the house until 1907. The workers seen here at the Martin House construction site would have had no previous experience with such a building. Its revolutionary design, pier and cantilever construction, relentless rectilinearity and unique combination of concrete, brick, wood, stone, glass and structural steel, distinguished the house from its more typical wood frame neighbors.

Restoration work at the Martin House in 2003 included stabilization of the Martin House foundation.

■ PAST NEGLECT AND RESTORED GLORY

Terra cotta roof tiles.

DECLINE AND DEGRADATION

Following Darwin Martin's death in 1935, his family suffered major financial setbacks and the Martin House began a tragic decline, with the family abandoning the house in 1937.

The Martin House stood open to the elements for more than a decade and suffered terribly from neglect and weather damage. Large numbers of windows were removed or sold off.

By the 1940's, demolition seemed imminent. Fortunately, in 1954, an architect, Sebastian Tauriello and his wife Ruth, purchased the property thus saving the Martin House from the same tragic fate that befell the Larkin Building in 1950. Ultimately the pergola, conservatory and carriage house were lost, along with the lush gardens that were once integral to the composition. Interior renovations altered Wright's original floor plan. The Tauriello family resided in the Martin House until 1966 when the State University of New York at Buffalo purchased it as a residence for its president who lived there until 1971. The University's stewardship brought the Martin House into a scholarly context with the beginning, in the 1970's, of public tours and academic gatherings. This era set the scene for the Martin House's future as a museum.

REBIRTH AND RESTORATION

Restoration of the Martin House Complex began in earnest in 1992 with the formation of the Martin House Restoration Corporation (MHRC), a not-for-profit organization charged with the mission to restore the house and open it as a museum. With the purchase of the Barton House, and the non-historic apartment buildings in 1994, the MHRC expanded its mission to include reconstruction of the missing elements – pergola, conservatory and carriage house – as well as the gardens and grounds. This represents the first Wright restoration with a mandate to reconstruct entirely demolished structures.

A CELEBRATION OF GENIUS

The Martin House was designated a National Historic Landmark in 1986, the highest accolade bestowed by the federal government for an historic site.

The Martin House Complex is considered one of Frank Lloyd Wright's finest residential designs of his Prairie House era (1901-1910), ranking in stature with the Robie House in Chicago and the Dana-Thomas House in Springfield, Illinois.

As an architectural masterpiece, the Martin House Complex stands as one of Wright's greatest works in the eastern United States, along with Fallingwater in Bear Run, Pennsylvania, and the Solomon R. Guggenheim Museum in New York City.

ROOF TILES

The first major phase in the Martin House Complex restoration occurred in 1998 when the Martin and Barton House roofs were repaired. A search for historically accurate terra cotta tiles led finally to Tuilerie de Pontigny Aléonard in Pontigny, France. A medieval kiln is employed there in the firing of clay tiles that possess the natural properties of the tiles that Wright originally specified for the Martin House Complex.

■ MARTIN HOUSE FACTS AND STATS

KEY TERMINOLOGY AND INFORMATION

The complex that encompasses both the Darwin D. Martin House and the George F. Barton House, as well as the grounds where the pergola, conservatory and carriage house will be reconstructed, is called the Martin House Complex.

The official name of the nonprofit organization that is restoring the Martin House Complex is the Martin House Restoration Corporation.

The MHRC office is located in downtown Buffalo, in the Theater District at the Market Arcade, 617 Main Street, Buffalo, New York 14203.

125 Jewett Parkway is the address of the Darwin D. Martin House.

118 Summit Avenue is the address of the George F. Barton House.

The original complete Martin House Complex was 29,080 sq. ft.
>   Darwin D. Martin House: 14,978 sq.ft.
>   Pergola: 1,540 sq.ft.
>   Conservatory: 2,655 sq.ft.
>   Carriage House: 5,507 sq.ft.
>   George Barton House: 4,400 sq.ft.

The Martin House Complex is a prime example of a Prairie House.

The National Historic Preservation Act (of 1966) created the National Register of Historic Places. The Darwin D. Martin House Complex has been on this list since 1975. The Martin House was named a National Historic Landmark in 1986.

The Martin House Complex is located within the Parkside East Historic District, which was placed on the National Register of Historic Places in 1986.

The Parkside Community was laid out by Frederick Law Olmsted in 1876 and was part of the first coordinated system of public parks in America.

Wasmuth Portfolio: Aüsgefuhrte Bauten und Entwürfe von Frank Lloyd Wright, a collection of Frank Lloyd Wright's most seminal drawings, was published in Berlin in 1910. The Martin House was included in this portfolio.

The Ginkgo, which is believed to be indigenous to Asia, was a favorite tree of Wright's.

Wright designed a floricycle to encircle the Martin House veranda. This semi-circular garden was comprised of a wide variety of plant species, chosen for their blossoming season to ensure a year-round bloom.

There are 394 art glass windows in the Martin House Complex in 15 distinct patterns. Though neither Wright nor Martin gave definitive names to any specific window, the most famous window, which is located throughout the second floor of the Martin House, has been referred to as the "Tree of Life" window for several decades.

The individual pieces of colored glass in these windows are surrounded by metal strips called came, or caming, which are then soldered together and fitted into metal frames, which in the Martin House are brass.

The two houses of the Complex are based on cruciform or cross-axial floor plans, an architectural motif widely seen in Gothic churches where the building is in the shape of a cross.

Frank Lloyd Wright was very keen on rectilinear structures that formed a straight line. The Martin House Complex was designed in this fashion allowing clear linear fields of vision throughout the various buildings.

The Darwin D. Martin and Frank Lloyd Wright Archive is located at the University Archives, University at Buffalo, State University of New York.

KEY PEOPLE

Frank Lloyd Wright b. June 8, 1867 d. April 9, 1959. Wright was born in Richland Center, Wisconsin

Martin Family

Darwin Denice {da-nīs} Martin b. October 25, 1865 d. December 17, 1935 in Bouckville, New York
Isabelle Minnie (Reidpath) Martin, his wife (married June 26, 1889) b. April 9, 1869 d. February 22, 1945
Dorothy Reidpath (Martin) Foster, their daughter b. June 27, 1896 d. February 1980
    James Forsyth Foster, Jr., her husband (married June 14, 1923)
    Margaret Reidpath Foster, their daughter b. January 31, 1930
    Darwin Martin Foster, their son b. November 11, 1930
Darwin Reidpath Martin, their son b. October 3, 1900 d. May 27, 1979
    Margaret (Wende) Martin, his first wife (married May 3, 1926)
    Laura (Bratnell) Martin, his second wife
    Alexander Martin, their son
    Patti (Martin) Arnesto, their daughter
    Millicent (Decker) Martin, his third wife (married 1975)

Delta Louise (Martin) Barton, Darwin's sister b. November 4, 1859
George Field Barton, her husband (married November 20, 1884) b. August 8, 1847 d. February 13, 1929

Laura Field (Barton) deForest, their daughter, d. October 18, 1892

KEY DATES

Darwin D. Martin and Frank Lloyd Wright agreed on Jewett Parkway for the site of the Martin's new home, and Martin acquired the property in November, 1902.

Building of the Complex began with the Barton House in 1903.

The Martin House was built primarily between 1903 and 1905.

The Martin family moved into the house in November, 1905.

The last craftsman did not leave the Martin House until 1907. [see pg. 28]

The "Year of Significance" for the restoration of the Martin House Complex is 1907, the year that the house was complete, the family was in residence, and no alterations had been made to Wright's design.

Sebastian Tauriello purchased the Martin House in 1955 (it had been abandoned since 1937).

The pergola, conservatory and carriage house were demolished in 1960.

In 1966, the Martin House was purchased by the University at Buffalo, State University of New York for use as its "president's house."

Eric and Eleanor Larrabee purchased the Barton House in 1967.

The Barton House was purchased from Eleanor Larrabee for the MHRC by M&T Bank, Rich Products Corp., and The Buffalo News in 1994.

Title to the Martin House was transferred by the University at Buffalo to the MHRC in 2002.

BUFFALO'S WRIGHTIAN GOLDEN AGE

For a golden age of some 22 years — from 1927 until 1949 — ten Wright-designed structures stood in and around Buffalo. That heyday included:

1.   George Barton House (1903-04), extant
2.   Larkin Company Administration Building (1904-06),
     demolished 1949-50
3.   Darwin D. Martin House (1904-05), extant,
     a National Historic Landmark
4.   Martin House Pergola (1903-05), demolished early 1960's
5.   Martin House Conservatory (1903-05), demolished early 1960's
6.   Martin House Carriage House and Stable (1903-05),
     demolished early 1960's
7.   William R. Heath House (1905), extant
8.   Martin House Gardener's Cottage (1908-09), extant
9.   Walter V. Davidson House (1908-09), extant
10. Martin family's lakeshore summer house, Graycliff
     (1926-27), extant

KEY RELATIONSHIPS

The Martin House Restoration Corporation is an Associate Member of the Frank Lloyd Wright Foundation.

In 2000, a Joint Cooperative Agreement was entered into among the MHRC, the University at Buffalo, State University of New York and the New York State Office of Parks, Recreation and Historic Preservation that set forth the organizational basis for restoring the Martin House Complex.

AFTERWORD

The Martin House belongs to all those who care deeply about it.

No group cares more deeply about the Martin House restoration, nor has been more central to its rebirth, than the hundreds of volunteers who are making this historic project a reality.

Martin House volunteers have generously poured their energies into this community-wide effort and continue to do so.

Among the many dedicated Martin House volunteers is Lesley Neufeld, who volunteered her services to compile, write and edit this volume.

May you thumb and ponder this book for many years to come. And may you have frequent occasion to visit the Darwin D. Martin House Complex and Graycliff in the years ahead.

— John C. Courtin
    Executive Director
    Martin House Restoration Corporation

ACKNOWLEDGEMENTS

The MHRC gratefully acknowledges the kind assistance of the archivists at the University Archives, University at Buffalo, State University of New York in assembling images for this book, and the Buffalo and Erie County Historical Society, and Biff Henrich, Keystone Film Productions, Inc.

Sincere thanks to Margaret P. Stehlik, Director, Martin House Volunteers, Dawn A. Warsaw, Assistant Director, *Restoration Campaign*, Mary F. Roberts, Director, Finance, Rebecca M. Lee, *Wisteria* Shop Manager, Eric Jackson-Forsberg, Associate Curator, and John C. Courtin, Executive Director, MHRC for their vision, support and encouragement of this project, and to Vince Benbenek for his incomparable design. Thanks also to Martin House Volunteer Judie Hillery for editorial comments and to Katy Delmonte for research.

PHOTOGRAPH SOURCES

Photographs are reprinted courtesy of the following:

University Archives, University at Buffalo, State University of New York: Cover, page 2, 3 [letters], 4, 5, 8, 10, 11, 13, 15, 18, 19, 20, 21, 22, 23, 24, 27, 28

Buffalo and Erie County Historical Society, page 1, page 25 [Larkin Building]

Collection of Frank Lloyd Wright Preservation Trust, H&S H273, cover, page 2 (Frank Lloyd Wright. Photographer unknown)

Biff Henrich, cover [upper right left], page 14, 16 [Tree of Life window], pages, 17, 21 [chair]

Anderson and Wahl, page 30 [roof tiles]

Martin House Restoration Corporation, page 3 [model], 4, 20 [stanchion], 26, 27 [Gardener's Cottage], 29

DRAWINGS

University Archives, University at Buffalo, State University of New York, page 25

"A Home in a Prairie Town", by Frank Lloyd Wright, *The Ladies' Home Journal*, February, 1901, illustration, page 5

Wasmuth Portfolio drawings by Frank Lloyd Wright from *Ausgeführte Bauten und Entwürfe von Frank Lloyd Wright* (Ernst Wasmuth, publisher, Berlin, 1910), Frank Lloyd Wright Foundation, page 6, 7, 9, 12,

TEXT

Quotations from "In the Cause of Architecture", by Frank Lloyd Wright, are reprinted with permission from *Architectural Record*, [Vol. XXIII, No. 3, 1908]

Excerpts from and copies of letters between Frank Lloyd Wright, Darwin D. and William Martin are from the collection of the University Archives, University at Buffalo, State University of New York.

MARTIN HOUSE RESTORATION CORPORATION
MARKET ARCADE, 617 MAIN ST, BUFFALO NY 14203-9857
716.856.3858 | www.darwinmartinhouse.org